176 WAYS TO INVOLVE PARENTS

Betty Boult

SkyLight
Professional
Development

Arlington Heights, Illinois

176 Ways to Involve Parents
Published by SkyLight Professional Development
2626 S. Clearbrook Dr., Arlington Heights, IL 60005
800-348-4474 or 847-290-6600
Fax 847-290-6609
info@skylightedu.com
http://www.skylightedu.com

Senior Vice President, Product Development: Robin Fogarty
Director, Product Development: Ela Aktay
Acquisitions Editor: Jean Ward
Project Coordinator: Amy Kinsman
Editor: Peggy Kulling
Book Designer: Dave Stockman
Cover Designer and Illustrator: David Stockman
Production Supervisor: Bob Crump
Proofreader: Ann Wilson
Indexer: Schroeder Indexing
Production Assistant: Christina Georgi

LCCCN 98-61832
ISBN 1-57517-153-8

2407V
Item Number 1721
ZYXWVUTSRQPONMLKJIHGFEDCB
07 06 05 04 03 02 01 00   15 14 13 12 11 10 9 8 7 6 5 4 3 2

Contents

Foreword   v

Preface   vii

Introduction   1

SECTION ONE

Making It Happen   **5**

     Jump Start the School Year: Involving Families   6

     Shared Interest: Supporting the Whole Family   8

     Recruiting Volunteers   11

     Meeting the Needs of Volunteers   14

     Facilitating a Full and Free Exchange of Ideas   16

     Comfort Food for Thought: Supporting Volunteers   21

     Acknowledging Volunteer Contributions   23

     Team Building: Learning to Work Together   26

SECTION TWO

Creating the Climate   **29**

     Sell the School: Projecting a Positive Image   30

     Marketing the Message   34

     Creating the Context for Change   38

     Affecting Substantive Change   40

     Random Selection: Ensuring Random Seating   43

     Getting to Know You: Establishing Connections   45

SECTION THREE

Sustaining the Involvement   **49**
    Utilizing Community Resources   50
    Share the Wealth: Training Volunteers   54
    Ensure Success: Placing Volunteers Appropriately 56
    Developing Collaborative Relationships   59
    Loud and Clear: Communicating Effectively   63

SECTION FOUR

Working in the Classroom   **67**
    Supporting Specific Initiatives   68
    Higher than Intellect: Building Character   71
    Creating Safe Havens for Students   74
    High Finance: Fundraising   77
    Talking Person to Person   80
    Celebrating Diversity   82

SECTION FIVE

Venturing Beyond the Bake Sale   **85**
    Collaboration and Consultation: Setting Goals   86
    Measuring Up: Evaluating School Performance   88
    Advice: Involving Those Affected by Decisions   90
    Fostering Effective Advisory Councils   92
    Developing Parent Potential   95
    District Initiatives: Setting the Example   99

Appendix   101
References   107
Index   109

SkyLight Training and Publishing Inc.

Foreword

176 Ways to Involve Parents addresses ways to best involve parents in their children's education. The public's demand for accountability has led educators to look for ways to most effectively work with parents. Naturally, the roles parents and educators play today will make for important differences in the future. Parent involvement is a timely subject and one educators and parents need to take very seriously because today's students will be tomorrow's citizens.

Betty Boult's book lays out the conditions required for constructive parent action in classrooms, schools, and districts. It demonstrates that parents should be involved in ways that suit themselves, their children, and the school. A multitude of activities are provided to promote parent participation, including providing classroom support, participating in district and school governance, offering community service, engaging in parent, student, and staff partnerships, and enriching curriculum.

176 Ways to Involve Parents is a handbook filled with practical ideas. These ideas will prove useful for educators and parents who seek proven practices that can be employed just as presented here or adapted to fit varying circumstances and preferences. The ideas range from ways to initiate parent involvement to ways to maintain that involvement by expanding volunteer opportunities and responsibilities. Some of the ideas can be readily implemented while others require more thorough preparation and sustained work. All of which are sure to enhance cooperation between home and school.

This insightful resource not only highlights the value of parent involvement but also shows it to be an integral part of education. Underlying each idea is the view that educators and parents are partners who have the same end in mind: the welfare of students. Betty Boult's message is an important one that is respectful of and values all partners in education.

There are both challenges and opportunities in the decades ahead, and parents, educators, and community leaders must fruitfully consider how they can best cooperate. Fortunately, *176 Ways to Involve Parents* provides excellent suggestions to do just that.

Herbert J. Walberg
Research Professor of
Education and Psychology
University of Illinois at Chicago

 SkyLight Training and Publishing Inc.

Preface

For the past thirty-two years, I have been involved in education in a number of different roles and locations—from classroom teacher to assistant superintendent. No matter where I have been, the topic of parents has always conjured up a variety of reactions from staff. As a beginning teacher, some of my colleagues told me how much I would enjoy the extra pair of hands, the skills parents brought to the classroom, and the insights parents would share about their children.

I was also told by other colleagues that parents were to be guarded against as they were unreasonable and wanted teachers to do everything for their children. Some stated that many parents did not assume responsibility for their children's actions. Above all, I was warned, parents could not be pleased. Many schools I worked in had minimal parent involvement and, in more than one situation, parents were treated as unwelcome intruders. Many staffs worked hard at keeping parents at a distance. Consequently, I became very interested in understanding the dynamics and impact of parent involvement. I believed I would provide quality education to children if I worked closely with parents. The ideas presented in this book have been gleaned from years of working with educators who have improved the quality of education for students by believing in and incorporating parent volunteers.

Society is undergoing an era of greater accountability with tremendous implications for education. I hope your school can benefit from the ideas in this book as you take up the challenges of the twenty-first century.

Betty Boult

Introduction

Power realignments in the educational arena have
always been a feature of the history of our public
schools, but it was only in the post-World War II era
that the question of "Who owns the schools?"
began to be raised....questions were being asked for
two related reasons: dissatisfaction with educational
outcomes, and challenges...to every major social
institution in the society. Undergirding all of these
questions was a moral-political one: who should
participate in educational decision making? And the
general answer was: any individual or group who
directly or indirectly would be affected by a decision
should stand in some relationship to the decision-
making process.

—*Seymour Sarasan (1990,53)*

Current research strongly supports the correlation between
the way school staff views parents and the quality of relationships within the school. Bruce Joyce and others (1993, 76)
acknowledge that parents want their children to be highly
educated citizens, and that it is up to educators "to make
parents part of our learning community, enlisting their energies
in our part of the growth and socialization of their children."
     In many schools, parents are welcomed as equal partners
in their child's education. Educators at such institutions
believe that making education a meaningful experience for
students requires a partnership; therefore, education is a
shared trust. The academic component is only a part of what

students need to be successful learners. Working in concert with parents to provide quality education to students is a necessity, not an option. The partnership of school and home needs to range from having parents check their children's homework to actively involving parents as key decision makers in the governance of the schools and the district. Herbert Walberg (1984, 399) observed that if teachers, parents, and students are equal partners in education, with each partner performing his or her role, a delicate balance can be struck. However, "if any one of these groups is unsupportive, little can be accomplished."

Two decades of research on student achievement validates the importance of involving parents. Alan Riley (1994) contended that students are advantaged when parents encourage and support their school activities. Suzanne Zeigler (1987, 14) stated, "Closer contact between home and school and greater involvement of parents in the education of their children are probably more important than educational administrators had generally realized."

The role of the parent in the operational system has been legitimized by major educational reforms, which in turn have defined parents' rights. Specifically, recent legislation in many jurisdictions has established an appeal process for the redress of parent and student grievances, access to records for parents, and a voice in the governance of the school system both at the school and district level. Furthermore, most parents no longer see themselves as passive players in education and have become vocal about the exercise of their rights. Laurence Iannacone (1975) asserted in his discussion of parent involvement that if issues pertaining to the delegation of decision-making power is not handled equitably by school boards, teachers unions, and administrators, then the support for public education will disappear. He went so far as to predict that a drastic restructuring of the way schools are governed will result. It is clear that parents must be afforded and empowered to have input into educational decisions.

To sum up, the relationship between parents and schools may be challenging and in some cases downright problematic.

However, the benefits of parent involvement have been proven. They include enhanced student self-esteem, increased academic achievement, and improved communication. Schools strengthen what they do by working collaboratively with parents.

176 Ways to Involve Parents is a hands-on guide for those who recognize the need and benefit of involving parents and is presented in five sections.

Section 1: Making It Happen focuses on ways to convey that decades of research has shown that by meaningfully involving parents, student learning is strengthened; parents become advocates instead of adversaries, and all partners have a sense of ownership of public education. It provides ideas on how to work with both the students and their families to involve them in the life of their school.

Section 2: Creating the Climate contains well thought out and practical methods of promoting and supporting communication and change. The section frames a plan for making the school aesthetically pleasing and inviting to the public. Readers are encouraged to laud their school's successes and programs by marketing their product, education, to the community it serves.

Section 3: Sustaining Involvement discusses how to effectively engage parents and the business community in shared ownership of the educational system. Ideas to enrich the quality of school life through encouraging, expecting, and supporting parent and business involvement are offered. Underlying the ideas is the belief that providing education to students is a shared responsibility and therefore all partners must have a role in its delivery.

Section 4: Working in the Classroom discusses methods by which schools can tap the great potential just waiting to be utilized in their community. Parents can contribute in a variety of ways. The ideas contained in this section center on providing opportunities for parents to bring their expertise to the classroom or to bring the classroom to the parents.

Section 5: Venturing Beyond the Bake Sale provides ample evidence that it is imperative that schools allow for meaningful parent involvement beyond their accepted and traditional role as fundraisers. Strategies for bringing about shared governance at the school and district levels are offered.

A "Background" discussion is included for each topic as a kind of pep talk and a call to action focusing on the importance of promoting a particular aspect of parent involvement. Several "Ideas to Use" are offered for each topic and reflect the most innovative research in the area of parent involvement in schools. "Points to Ponder" are cautions and comments on the ideas and reinforce the indisputable case for a partnership with parents.

SECTION ONE

Making It Happen

Effectively engaging
parents and families in the
education of their children
has the potential to be far
more transformational than
any other type of education
reform.

*—PTA National Standards for Parent/Family
Involvement Programs (1997,5)*

The key to parent involvement is demonstrating to parents
that the school wants them to be a part of school life. The
ways parents can be involved are endless and the need for
their involvement is pressing. All involvement is important,
whether it be at home with parental support of a child's
academic progress, in the classroom, or on advisory councils.
Schools must value whatever time commitment parents make
and recognize that most parents want to support their children
but are not always clear on how to make a difference. Educators must convey to parents that their involvement is essential
to the learning process.

Jump Start the School Year: Involving Families

Background

Create an atmosphere that gives the message that the family and the school need to work together. Offering opportunities where everyone can be involved in a nonthreatening and supportive environment creates a culture of community.

Ideas to Use

1. Begin the school year with a celebration.

Convert your traditional September parent-teacher meeting into an evening where the whole family is invited. Include any event or activity that helps parents understand the importance of the family relationship with the school. Consider hosting a barbecue or organizing a flea market. Make sure to have a sign-up booth for school volunteers. Plan activities and events that facilitate staff introductions.

2. Prepare a welcome package to distribute to new families.

Include business promotions (discounts on pizza or dry

SkyLight Training and Publishing Inc.

cleaning provided by local merchants), maps of the school and town, and folders and pencils emblazoned with the school name and logo. Sample newsletters and the names of advisory council members should also be included to make parents aware of how the school communicates with its families. Include a list of ways parents can be involved in the life of the school as well. Make sure the list is also handed out at registration.

3. Offer home visits.

Ask parents if they are interested in having one of the other parents in the community drop in to visit them at home. The advisory council can organize and train a group of parents who are interested in helping new families. The visiting parents should discuss community and school resources. Making sure that the visiting parent shares the same language or culture as the parent they are calling on promotes greater communication, comfort, and inclusion.

4. Survey families at the beginning of the year to identify the expertise in the school community.

Find out more about parent interests, hobbies, travels, and jobs. Then, ask parents to share their experiences with the school either at career day programs or as curriculum resource speakers.

Points to Ponder

All of these activities need coordination and planning. Divide the tasks up so there is shared responsibility between staff members and the advisory council. Involve students in appropriate activities such as assembling the welcome packages.

Shared Interest: Supporting the Whole Family

Background

> The way schools care about children is re-
> flected in the way schools care about the
> children's families. If educators view children
> simply as students, they are likely to see the
> family as separate from the school.... Partners
> recognize their shared interests in and respon-
> sibilities for children, and they work together
> to create better programs and opportunities
> for students.
>
> —*Joyce Epstein (1995, 703)*

Events that are focused on building the concept of family create opportunities to develop positive relations among the entire school community. Involvement of parents, students, community members, and organizations is crucial to the success of such efforts. Relating to students as whole persons with lives outside of school necessitates supporting the family. Therefore, helping the family helps the student.

SkyLight Training and Publishing Inc.

Ideas to Use

5. Sponsor a family goods exchange.

Include items such as skates, skis, winter boots, and parkas.

6. Host book fairs.

7. Promote family literacy by staging a family reading night.

8. Offer English as a Second Language (ESL) classes to parents and others in the community.

Work with your local community college for best results.

9. Provide coping with grief sessions for students and their families.

Too many young persons today suffer from having lost a loved one or friend to violence. Families need support in dealing with depression brought on by unresolved or unaddressed grief issues. School social workers and psychologists can help organize the sessions.

10. **Foster a support group for single parents.**

Allow the group to meet at the school. Offer in-kind contributions by advertising their meetings and allowing facilitators the use of the photocopier and other office machines.

11. **Facilitate parent get-togethers.**

This strategy is particularly helpful to language or cultural minority parents. Because language minority students are less likely to participate in sports and other extracurricular activities, their parents are afforded fewer opportunities for interaction with other parents. Offer school facilities for a parent wine and cheese night; pancake breakfast, car rally, or other social-based activities.

Points to Ponder

Encourage cooperation between the partner groups (which could include police, social service agencies, staff, parents, and students) in planning, implementing, and evaluating the events. Make sure to plan them well enough in advance so that they can be included in the annual school calendar.

SkyLight Training and Publishing Inc.

Recruiting Volunteers

Background

Recruitment of parent volunteers should be an on-going activity that is not done in isolation. Be proactive and realistic when building the number of parents who are involved. Make sure parents and the community know that the school has an open-door policy. Such a policy needs to be supported by demonstrating that when parents come to the school to discuss issues or concerns, or simply to visit, they feel welcome and that their needs will be addressed as soon as possible.

Ideas to Use

12. Advertise year-round for volunteers.

Make requests for both general assistance and for help with specific activities or events. More volunteers will be attracted if they know what their potential roles will be. Clearly define and advertise the expectations for parent volunteers. Tasks should be clearly outlined and include a time component. Be prepared to offer alternative volunteer activities. Keep in mind that some parents may not be able to come to school to help but would be willing to undertake tasks they could do at home.

13. Employ a structured approach to involving parents.

Select volunteers by geographic location or draft every fifth parent alphabetically.

14. Use as much personal contact as possible to inform parents of volunteer opportunities and to invite them to participate.

Use handwritten notes by students and telephone calls.

15. Advertise the need for volunteers in community and business newsletters.

Ask the local chamber of commerce, grocery stores, real estate agencies, and doctors and dentists offices for space on their bulletin boards, newsletters, and Web sites.

16. Offer job sharing.

Time commitments may curtail parent involvement. Offer the opportunity for parents to share a volunteer assignment. A mother with a newborn at home may not be able to commit to a three hour stretch as library parent, but may be able to give an hour and a half with the remainder of the shift staffed by another parent. Facilitate interaction between parents so that such arrangements may be made.

SkyLight Training and Publishing Inc.

17. **Consider employing a full-time trained volunteer coordinator for your district or school.**

Having such a position has been shown to have a tremendous impact on the level of volunteer participation and the quality and productivity of volunteer programs (Bembry 1996). Otherwise, recruit a parent who is willing to make the substantial commitment of serving as volunteer coordinator. Provide parents with the appropriate training and resources, such as access to support staff and office supplies.

18. **Hold a volunteer fair.**

Have booths that represent various volunteer programs. Include a booth for the PTA and another for the Parent Boosters Club, for instance. Advertise the fair to the entire community. Hold it in conjunction with another school event, such as a football homecoming game, that is likely to attract parents, students, and alumni.

Points to Ponder

Broaden requests for involvement to social service agencies, senior citizen homes, high schools, colleges, and businesses. Do not turn down a prospective helper. Allow for flexibility in scheduling of activities and events to accommodate the schedules of volunteers.

Meeting the Needs of Volunteers

Background

It is not enough to recruit parents and community members to assist at the school. It is necessary for educators to make a conscious effort to meet the needs of individuals who are giving of their time. Create a school climate where volunteers have a sense of belonging. Parents need to feel they are welcomed and supported.

Ideas to Use

19. **Meaningfully involve volunteers in planning, evaluating, and implementing programs and projects.**

However, keep the parent volunteers' level of involvement in a range that is comfortable for both volunteers and staff.

20. **Motivate parents to remain involved by ensuring that volunteer tasks are interesting and challenging.**

SkyLight Training and Publishing Inc.

21. **Evaluate volunteer performance and give appropriate feedback.**

Know the volunteers well enough to tailor the form of the evaluation to the needs of the specific volunteer. A volunteer self-evaluation can help define the role performed by that individual and communicate a volunteer's impressions of the school and the assignment. All evaluations and feedback should be constructive and seek to promote growth and understanding.

Points to Ponder

The most effective way to meet the needs of volunteers is to know what volunteers need. Do this by getting to know the community from which volunteers will potentially come. Successful volunteer programs are those that proactively try to eliminate barriers to parent participation wherever possible.

Facilitating a Full and Free Exchange of Ideas

Background

Most parents have a vision of what they want for their children's education; however, they may not be able to effectively communicate that vision. Correspondingly, teachers and administrators need to share what they believe to be the optimum teaching and learning situation. Therefore, it is important to provide an opportunity for parents and staff to discuss what constitutes an effective learning environment for students. In order to involve parents, be sure to demonstrate that parent opinions are valued.

Ideas to Use

22. Begin with the abstract.

Divide parents into groups and have each group design a mock advertisement for an ideal school. Share the ads from the different groups. Identify the commonalities between the ads. The activity promotes discussion of parents' beliefs about education and can be a springboard for goal setting.

23. Hats off to good ideas.

Post large pieces of chart paper around the room. At the top of each sheet write a general heading related to one of the topics on which you want parent input. (The same heading can be repeated a number of times.) Divide each sheet into two columns. On the left side draw a black hat and on the right side draw a yellow hat. Ask parent and staff participants to write their concerns, issues, and challenges under the black hat. Strengths, compliments, and suggestions should go under the yellow hat. Don't have more than three or four parents working at one time on a sheet. Gauge the number of sheets you put up according to the number of participants. Limit discussion to five topics at any one meeting.

24. Fill in the blank.

Have parents complete the following sentences at a meeting, through a class or school newsletter, or by a telephone survey.

- The school is best known for . . .
- If I had a magic wand, I would change the school by . . .
- I could be involved in the school in the following manner . . .
- The best way of communicating with me as a parent is . . .
- We (the school, the district, parents) do_____ really well.
- Our school needs to _____ differently.

25. Attach a "Beefs and Bouquets" section to each newsletter.

Be prepared to deal with the criticisms as well as the compliments. Complete the advice cycle by responding to those that sign their comments. (See The Advice Cycle diagram, below.)

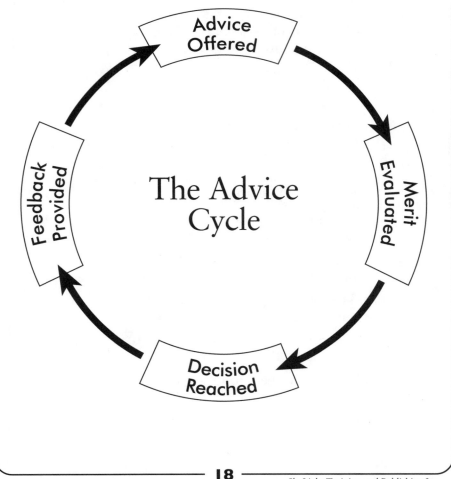

The Advice Cycle

Advice Offered

Merit Evaluated

Decision Reached

Feedback Provided

SkyLight Training and Publishing Inc.

26. **Monitor how inviting it is to be a member of the school community.**

A school community (parents, staff, and students) should discuss the following questions:

- How do staff and students greet visitors?
- How are new staff, students, and parents welcomed into the school community?
- Is there a welcoming plan in place or does it just happen by chance?
- Are students, parents, and/or staff asked when they are leaving how they felt about the school as a community?
- Are they asked what they most enjoyed and what they would change?
- Are the contributions of each parent group acknowledged equitably?

27. **Toe the line.**

Make two lines of chairs facing each other, directly across from one another. As parents arrive, hand them either a piece of paper with a plus sign (+) or a minus sign (-). All persons with minus signs sit on one side and all persons with plus signs sit on the other. There needs to be a minimum of ten persons to do this exercise effectively. The person with the plus sign has to present the benefits of the topic to the person sitting across from him or her (toeing the other side of the line) while the person with the minus sign has to listen quietly. Each person then moves three seats to the right and the exercise is repeated, but this time the plus sign presents the cons and the minus sign states the pros. Do this no more than three times. Then have the participants break up into groups of four (two plus signs and two minus signs) and develop a position statement on the topic at hand.

Points to Ponder

Keep in mind that six is the optimum size for any group activity. Structure ways to respond to parent input or parents will stop providing it. Each of the strategies should be implemented in such a way as to make parent participation easy. If the request is too complicated, there will be fewer responses.

SkyLight Training and Publishing Inc.

Comfort Food for Thought: Supporting Volunteers

Background

Parents do not always have the time or resources to be involved in their child's education. Therefore, the time parents are involved should be time well and meaningfully spent. Schools that recognize parent barriers to involvement and make a concerted effort to reach parents benefit from increased involvement and support. Such efforts enhance the belief that the staff wants parents to be involved.

Ideas to Use

28. **Provide free child care to encourage parents to come to school activities.**

Be clear about where the children are to meet, who will be attending them, what entertainment will be provided, and hours of operation. Provide a contact name and number so spots can be reserved.

29. Facilitate baby-sitting pools for parents who want to spend some time volunteering in the school.

30. Provide refreshments to volunteers to engender a feeling of comfort.

31. Offer transportation alternatives to parents without cars.

Facilitate car pools. When an invitation is made to come to school it should include transportation options (local bus routes and times as well as numbers to call for a ride). Check to see if the district bus service can run a special route for parents when activities are being held at school that parents should attend.

Points to Ponder

The child care activities are ones that advisory councils are often interested in coordinating and can lead to a positive working relationship between the council and student leaders in the school. In the staff lounge, listing the accumulated weekly or monthly total number of volunteer hours to date will build morale and is a visible representation of the level of volunteer commitment.

Acknowledging Volunteer Contributions

Background

It is important to positively reinforce parents by acknowledging their role in the school. Parents volunteer their time to improve the quality of school life. Procedures should be in place that make parents feel welcome and demonstrate that parent opinions and contributions are valued. Recognition is an important part of involving parents because if they do not feel appreciated, they will not stay involved. Acknowledgment does not require a major effort, but will have a major payoff.

Ideas to Use

32. Catch parents in the act of volunteering.

Use the school camera or yearbook photographer to take pictures of parents as they are involved in a volunteer assignment. Find appropriate ways to display the pictures. Create a photo collage, a slide show, or a video for the final appreciation event. Utilize bulletin boards to express appreciation and show who is involved.

Remember: photos always make a nice marketing presentation for new recruits.

33. **Acknowledge and profile parent volunteers in the school newsletters and yearbook.**

34. **Recognize a volunteer of the month or week.**

35. **Hold an annual recognition event.**
The event could take the form of a luncheon, tea, or dinner. Consider an all-school assembly where parents are honored through skits and songs. Present volunteers with tokens of appreciation, maybe ones made by students.

36. **Replace visitors' buttons or tags with "VIP" buttons.**
It will certainly convey the message that volunteer contributions are important.

37. **Send personalized "thank you" notes.**
Make sure a system is in place to do this, whether it is the responsibility of the volunteer coordinators, the administration, or an individual.

38. **Feature parent volunteers and their contributions as a regular item on the school or district Web site.**

39. **Put a different class in charge of honoring volunteer efforts each month.**

Points to Ponder

The demonstration of appreciation needs to be a clearly stated school or district objective to ensure it is not overlooked. Seek parent input to determine relevant and meaningful displays of appreciation.

Team Building: Learning to Work Together

Teamwork necessitates that persons be thoughtful and considerate of others. Individuals working effectively together need a sense that they are valued as individuals as well as members of the team. When they feel valued, they are more willing to become interdependent with other members of a team.

Ideas to Use

40. **Follow the bouncing ball.**

The activity needs to be done with a group of persons who work together. In addition, it would be a good activity for an advisory council meeting just prior to a holiday. The chairperson of the meeting hands out a sheet of paper to each participant. The handout asks for information based on six personal questions.

- What is your favorite beverage?
- What is your favorite color?
- What is your favorite activity when you have free time?
- What is your favorite television show?
- What is your favorite holiday spot?
- What is your favorite food?

26

Participants write their names on the paper. Then, have everyone stand in a circle and scrunch the sheet with his or her answers on it into a ball and throw it. Everyone keeps picking up the papers and throwing them until the chairperson tells them to stop. Each person picks up a "scrunched ball" and opens it.

They are to keep the name of the person's ball they have a secret. Their responsibility is to do something nice for that person by a specific time. If a person picks up his or her own sheet, the chairperson needs to organize an exchange.

41. Conduct a human treasure hunt.

With a little revision, the same questions asked in number 40 above can be used. Hand out the following questions to persons as they walk in the door and ask them to search for persons whose . . .

- favorite beverage is lemonade?
- favorite color is blue?
- favorite activity is hiking?
- favorite TV show is *Frasier*?
- favorite holiday spot is in Mexico?
- favorite food is pizza?

Have them sign the sheet and hand it in when they have completed it. Draw two or three names and award small prizes (a school pen, box of candy, or plant).

42. Color coordinate the discussion.

Post chart paper with a different band of color (red, yellow, green, and blue) at each corner of the room before the meeting begins. Assign a discussion topic to each color. As parents enter the room, hand them a colored piece of paper (red, yellow, green, or blue). Assign a discussion topic to each color. Individuals gather at the appropriate chart and discuss the topic for a maximum of ten minutes. Plan for anywhere from forty to sixty minutes for this activity depending on the number of charts the groups are asked to visit. Within each of the color groups, ask the individual wearing the most of that particular color to report three key insights. Each color group must decide what is to be reported to the group as a whole. The facilitator charts the insights on the overhead. The group then moves to another color/topic and repeats the activity. If there is time during the session, it is better to have groups go to all charts so they feel they have had input on all issues. Compile the insights as feedback and circulate to those who were in attendance.

Points to Ponder

Use the above tactics at workshops, advisory council meetings, and parent education sessions. Wisdom is not the prerogative of the few and the school will benefit from collective thinking.

SkyLight Training and Publishing Inc.

SECTION TWO

Creating the Climate

Collaboration becomes a
central feature of the
leadership role and of the
culture of the school. In
moving to this position
the administration builds
on trust and fosters
mutual respect between
teachers and parents
from all groups. As teachers and parents engage in
discussing the needs of the learner, and school and
home are more closely integrated, the results in
student achievement are dramatic.

—*Alan Riley (1994, 188)*

The key to effectively working with parents is the establishment of a climate that values parental involvement as an integral part of a successful educational system. A system that is truly collaborative has a variety of infrastructures in place from the boardroom to the classroom that facilitate such an enterprise. Christine Emmons (1995) points out that frequent meaningful interactions between parents and the school is an indication of how well a school functions.

Creating an accepting climate requires trust among students, teachers, support staff, parents, and administrators. To create such a climate of trust, there must be a concerted effort made at all levels of the organization.

Sell the School: Projecting a Positive Image

Background

Develop a specific marketing plan that will show the school in a positive light. Be clear about the school or district's objectives when planning marketing strategies. Make certain that any marketing plan highlights the school's role in the academic, social, emotional, aesthetic, and physical development of students and the community.

Ideas to Use

43. **Create a physical atmosphere in the school and grounds that is friendly and inviting.**

Offer reading material and comfortable chairs in reception areas; extensively display student work, and hang "welcome" signs in languages that are appropriate for the community. Install a marquee to advertise upcoming events and recognize student and teacher accomplishments for the whole neighborhood to see.

44. **Invite two or three community members (alumni and business leaders) who do not have children in the school system to visit the school and do an informal audit.**

Ask the auditors the following questions after they tour the facility:

- What is your initial impression of the school?
- Did you feel comfortable coming to the school?
- Were there friendly faces, helpful staff, and students?
- How do the facilities and grounds rate in terms of cleanliness, signage, and availability of parking?
- What other observations do you have?

Have them meet with a representative partner group (teachers, parents, students, and administrators) to discuss their findings. Ask them if they have suggestions for improvement. Discuss with the auditors what procedure will be used to further share and act on their findings.

45. Offer articulation meetings for parents of matriculating students.

Articulation meetings are designed to ease the transition for students moving from one school to another, from elementary to middle school for instance. The middle school administrators, in this case, along with relevant staff, host a parent meeting at the elementary school where expectations of parents and staff may be "articulated." Include school tours as part of the articulation process.

46. Welcome mid-year transfers.

Devise your own brand of "welcome wagon." Provide new parents and students with information on the surrounding community as well as on the school. The materials can be sent through the mail, or schedule a courtesy call to a new arrival's home. Representatives of the advisory council, school counselors, or an administrator should conduct the home visit.

47. Offer adult programs during the school day.

Work with the district's continuing education department or that of the local community college to determine appropriate course offerings, which may include cooking, fitness, and skill-enhancement classes. Be aware that parents may perceive student safety issues. Deal with their concerns in an up-front and forthright manner.

48. Involve students in community projects.

Have students provide services to senior citizens (cutting lawns, shopping for groceries, running errands); volunteer in public institutions such as libraries, hospitals, and hospices; support community initiatives such as reclaiming parkland and restocking lakes.

49. Develop a "Beautify the School" plan.

The advisory council may wish to sponsor classroom planters that teachers can integrate into science units. These planters can eventually become part of a school garden.

SkyLight Training and Publishing Inc.

50. **Prepare an enrollment information package.**

In addition to general school information, include age-appropriate games, staff biographies, recipes for items such as homemade play dough, and school trivia questions that point up the unique character of the school.

51. **Create a video starring the school.**

Encourage middle or secondary school students through their electives to create the video or consider having a professional produce it. Make multiple copies of the final product and disseminate to appropriate parties such as business partners, the chamber of commerce, and local realtors. Show the video at parent-teacher conferences, articulation evenings, and other community events hosted by the school. Show it at malls, car dealerships, or any other accessible public venue.

Points to Ponder

Marketing should be an expressed part of the school and district's action plans. Remember that nothing makes a school look better than polite, well-mannered, and contributing students.

Marketing the Message

Background

> Educators must reach out to parents and members of the public...our most pressing need is to reestablish public support for the public schools.
>
> —*Ron Brandt (1998, 26)*

There is no question that educators must constantly communicate that wonderful teaching and learning takes place every day in schools. The problem educators face is that the public is not as informed as they should be about the quality job the public education system is doing. What's more, public consensus is needed to approve bond issues to fund schools. Unfortunately, the majority of the public cannot see the need for additional funding because they are unaware of what is taking place within schools. Educators need to take responsibility for communicating and be more proactive in doing so. Continually inform the public about what is going well and what challenges the school is facing.

Ideas to Use

52. Establish contact with the local media.

Invite members of the media to all school events. Don't forget to provide invitations to events with an academic focus, like science fairs and college bowl competitions, as well as sporting events. Include media representatives in volunteer appreciation efforts during the course of the year or plan a separate media-relations lunch.

53. Use volunteers to help distribute programs, bulletins, and newsletters door-to-door around the school's neighborhood several times a year.

Remember a majority of the residents of the community do not have children in school. Share the school's successes, goals, and plans.

54. Assemble a photomontage of the year showing programs or projects in progress.

It could take the form of a memory book or a classroom or hall display. Include a variety of shots from academic endeavors to community service. Ask parents throughout the year to make doubles of pictures they take at school events and donate those doubles to the school. Display the photos in a place where the whole school and its visitors may enjoy them.

55. Read the handwriting on the wall.

Place large graffiti sheets (chart paper or newsprint) on the walls in an area to which parents have access such as the office reception area, hallway, or foyer. Have marking pens available for ad hoc parent comments. Consider focusing the input each week by having specific headings on the graffiti sheets.

56. **Foster discussion about education as a classroom teacher.**

Survey parents on the following topics:

- What concerns do you have about your child's education?
- What are the strengths of the education system in relation to your child's education?
- What do you expect from a classroom teacher?
- How do you keep your child accountable for his or her learning?
- What is your role in your child's schooling?
- How does your child learn best?

Remember to respond to parent comments.

57. **Publish and circulate a classroom newsletter reporting the activities specific to that class or homeroom.**

Include suggestions for helping with homework and a "Coming Up" section to get parents and students ready for the next chapter or topic.

58. **Create a class home page as a link from the school or district Web site.**

Include the same kind of information that would be included in a class newsletter as above but update more frequently. Give daily homework tips. Suggest other Web sites to explore. Not only is this a good way to use all that technology has to offer, but it can also serve as an entre´ for a discussion of Internet safety for young people.

Points to Ponder

Use the strategies above to demonstrate to parents that educators are more than willing to discuss education with them and that the school doesn't have all the answers but is willing to learn from parents. As a result, the enhanced and improved communication will benefit all parties.

Creating the Context for Change

Background

Schools must not only change and grow themselves; they must encourage change and growth in the community they serve. Most persons do not like change and are thus unable to consider alternatives to a current method of operation. It is important to create a context for change and establish some common understandings among and between schools and parents.

Ideas to Use

59. Pick a number.

In groups of six to eight, brainstorm five words or ideas under the following headings: Language, Values, Inventions, and Parenting. Give the group ten to fifteen minutes to list items that underscore what is different today as compared to twenty years ago. The facilitator selects one word under each column. For example, use the word number 2 under Language, use the word number 4 under Values, use the word number 5 under Inventions, and number 3 under Parenting.

SkyLight Training and Publishing Inc.

Have the group use these words to write a statement about change. Allow them to be funny or serious. Hand out long strips of paper and have each group write the statement out, sign their names to it, and post it on the wall. As the participants break for refreshments, they can circulate and read the other groups' statements.

60. Connect the variables.

Each parent is asked to reflect upon the relationship between student achievement and the following: teachers' expectations, parents' expectations, economic status, parental involvement, and attendance. Have them discuss their comments in groups of four. Then, have the groups formulate a statement about student achievement. Share with those assembled that research has found parent involvement to be the single most demonstrative factor relating to student success at all levels (Henderson and Berla 1994).

Points to Ponder

Parents often need a chance to voice their concerns and hear other points of view before they are willing to discuss possible solutions. Remember that a person's perception is his or her truth.

Affecting Substantive Change

Background

Parents, like everyone else, see the world not as it is but as they are. One's perceptions are key to accepting change. Michael Fullan and Matthew Miles (1992) said that if change is truly substantive, individuals involved in the change will deal with it by giving it personal meaning. An atmosphere that acknowledges the difficulties involved in accepting change and that encourages risk-taking is crucial to the evolution of thought and therefore to growth.

40

Ideas to Use

61. Throw them a lifeline.

Have participants in groups of six to eight use a horizontal line as their lifeline from birth to their current age. Vertical lines should be drawn at appropriate places on the line to mark key events in their respective lives. Use at a meeting where some change in education that may be controversial and require parental support is to be discussed. Ask which life events most affected participant's attitudes towards education. Have them discuss change as a group. Relate the personal changes in life to the changes faced in education.

62. Launch a time capsule.

Include items such as student compositions about the school and community, school pins, artwork, and predictions about what the school and community will be like in twenty-five years. Host a community ceremony where the time capsule is sealed. Bury it in an appropriate location. This activity helps individuals focus on the fact that change is a constant condition of life.

63. Employ a Venn diagram to initiate a discussion about change.

Label two overlapping circles "Schools 20 Years Ago" and "Schools Today" respectively. Ask participants to work in groups of three to define the area of intersection, which should represent the commonalities between the two eras. Allow fifteen to twenty minutes for the completion of the diagrams, and then ask the groups to share their work. List the various groups' responses. (See Venn Diagram.)

Venn Diagram

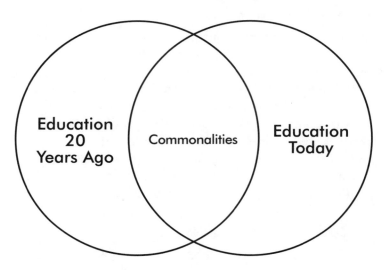

Points to Ponder

Often comparing the way things were to the way they are now and seeing what the commonalities are helps parents discuss and clarify issues they may have regarding change. Thus, the above activities create the correct context, or mindset, to discuss educational change. In addition, the ideas offer a way to lead from a general discussion on change to a specific issue that needs to be addressed.

Random Selection: Ensuring Random Seating

Background

On some occasions it is important that parents mix and do not just sit with the same group of persons they know. Random seating stimulates a cross-fertilization of ideas and opens discussion.

Ideas to Use

64. Get it together.

Enlarge five cartoons to 8^1/$_2$- by 11-inch size using a photocopier with enlargement capability. Cut each cartoon into six pieces. The number of cartoons will depend on the number of groups to be created. As parents arrive, hand them a piece of a cartoon. They have to find the five other persons that have the pieces of the same cartoon and form a group. On each table, have a glue stick and a felt pen. Have the group glue the cartoon on a sheet of paper and write a caption under it relating to the topic of the meeting. Once they have finished, have each group post their cartoon at the front of the room and then sit together in their group.

43

65. Spill the beans.

Have different colored jelly beans (groups of six of the same color) in a dish. Have each person take a jelly bean as they come in the door. A person sits in a group at the table that has a dish of jelly beans matching the color he or she has selected. As parents join the group, have each person introduce him or herself to the other members.

Points to Ponder

Often when parents come to a meeting they come with someone they know and do not like to be separated from them. Know that the above activities take people out of their comfort zones and make it "risky" for some. Therefore, it is important to link these activities to the main content of the session or participants will perceive these activities as a waste of time.

SkyLight Training and Publishing Inc.

Getting to Know You: Establishing Connections

Background

When a group of individuals (staff and parents) that do not know each other come together for discussion, structure ways to have them meet that are not threatening. When a person is put at ease and welcomed as part of a group, that person will contribute more than a person left at the outskirts of a meeting.

Ideas to Use

66. Back to back.

Have participants partner with someone in the room they do not know. Provide each person with a sheet of paper and a pen. Have them spend a few minutes talking about why they happen to be at the meeting and what their perceived role is there. After a couple of minutes, have them sit back to back and answer the following questions about their respective partners:

- How tall is the person?
- What color are his or her eyes?
- What jewelry does the person have on?
- Does the person wear glasses?
- What is the person wearing?

Have them turn around and check their memories. Use this as an opener to talk about first impressions, memories, the way they communicated when they met. Have them debrief and use the exercise as a platform to talk about perceptions and communication.

67. Take three.

Ask participants to introduce themselves to someone with whom they are not acquainted in the room using only three items found on their person. For example: a child's photograph, a scarf, and a briefcase. If a person does not have three items, they may use "imagined" items.

68. Play twenty questions.

Have persons pair up with individuals they do not know. Tell them they must be prepared to introduce the person to the group by discerning the following information:

The person's name

Where they live; and,

Four or five interesting facts about the person.

The interviewers are limited to asking only twenty questions of their subject, and their subject may only respond to the questions with a yes or no answer.

SkyLight Training and Publishing Inc.

After they have each had the opportunity to ask the twenty questions, they introduce each other to the group using the information they obtained from the yes/no responses.

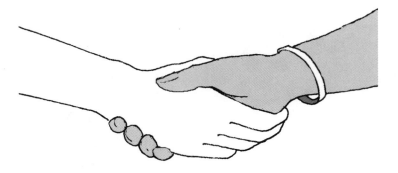

Points to Ponder

At the beginning of a meeting put participants at ease by having them spend a few minutes getting to know each other. Educators are constantly in meetings but most parents are not. Therefore, be sensitive to the fact that parents may feel apprehensive about participating as part of a group.

SECTION THREE

Sustaining the Involvement

[Schools] are much more successful when they blur distinctions between the professional and lay community and involve [those they serve] wherever possible in the functions of the organization.

— *Bruce Joyce, James Wolf, and Emily Calhoun (1993,76)*

Difficulties related to parental involvement (such as declining numbers of parent volunteers, frustration with roles, unresolved conflict, and dissatisfaction with the school) occur when educators do not meaningfully involve parents. Because some teachers and administrators do not want parents to interfere in what they see as the professional's domain, parents are often kept at an arm's length. To ensure that parents and community members are genuinely and meaningfully involved, schools must establish structures that train, support, and acknowledge volunteer contributions.

Utilizing Community Resources

Background

There are unlimited resources in a school community and a wide range of expertise that can be utilized to promote learning. It follows then that by combining the wide range of skills, talents, and resources the community can offer with those of parents and teachers, the learning process is enhanced and enriched.

Ideas to Use

69. Ask parents and other interested members of the community to coach extra-curricular clubs during lunch hour or after school.

70. Model good citizenship.

Have student leaders approach the owner or manager of a grocery store and see if he or she will agree to the following proposal. For every $1,000 worth of receipts from that establishment that the students' collect during a specified period of time, the store contributes $10 to a community food bank. Many parents would be more than willing to work with students to coordinate the project.

71. Hold a blind auction.

Ask the parent and business community to contribute items for the auction. Be clear about how the funds raised will be used.

72. Organize a pizza night.

Partner with a local pizza place and designate a particular night as pizza night. Provide the business with advertising for the event and have the business respond by returning fifteen to twenty percent of the sales as a donation to the school.

73. Include the senior members of the community.

"Adopt" seniors so that the school can share its resources and seniors can share theirs. Have seniors discuss their life stories from a historical perspective. Students could interview, write journals, or create videos of the experiences shared with the seniors. In return, students could teach interested seniors how to use computers. Ask seniors to tutor students either at school or at senior centers. Offer a student reading service for seniors in return.

74. Offer free admission for senior citizens to school events such as sporting events and school plays.

75. Organize safety patrols on Halloween night.

Volunteers could either patrol in well-marked vehicles or on foot from five o'clock to nine o'clock. This will help prevent school and community vandalism as well as protect the younger children from potential harassment. Coordinate efforts with that of the local police force. Give the volunteers treats to hand out as they patrol the streets.

76. Create a resource directory.

Start with the Yellow Pages of the local telephone book and list those community resources (businesses, services, and governmental organizations) that could be utilized during the course of the year as a source of volunteers, sponsors, or visitation hosts. Survey the staff members to see which resources they have used in the past and include the best sources in the directory. Keep track of how often a particular resource is used to prevent overtaxing that source's generosity.

77. Visit parents' job sites on field trips.

Government offices, retail stores, hospitals, factories, universities, farms, banks, schools, and nursing homes are just some examples of trips that align well with curriculum. Have the parent conduct the tour when possible.

78. Incorporate elements of the community into the curriculum.

If a unit on pioneers is being taught, then elicit cooperation from the city or municipal office in allowing students to mock file for sections of land like original homesteaders.

SkyLight Training and Publishing Inc.

Points to Ponder

Many businesses are more than willing to help and simply need to be approached; while, involving seniors acknowledges their valuable contributions as citizens. Working with the larger community reinforces the principle that everyone is involved in education. Certainly, in this day and age, it is more clear than ever that "it takes a village to raise a child."

Share the Wealth: Training Volunteers

Background

Orient and train volunteers to ensure they are comfortable in their roles, feel competent at their assigned responsibilities, and know they are valued. In addition, present the volunteer program as an opportunity for volunteers themselves to gain skills and experience.

Ideas to Use

79. **Host an orientation session for volunteers.**

Conduct a school tour and be sure each volunteer is introduced to every staff member.

80. **Develop a code of ethics for volunteers with input from the teaching staff and volunteers themselves.**

Focus on confidentiality issues such as discussing individual student's progress and student records and health and safety issues, such as the prohibition of smoking and drinking on school grounds.

SkyLight Training and Publishing Inc.

81. **Publish a volunteer handbook.**

Clarify the role of volunteers. Enunciate expectations such as attendance and confidentiality. Provide relevant information such as volunteer sign-in procedures, conflict resolution strategies, and methods of evaluation. In addition, be sure volunteers receive the school safety procedures, student disciplinary code, volunteers' code of ethics, and a map of the building and grounds.

82. **Provide ongoing training for volunteers on topics such as teaching styles, conflict resolution, instructional technology, and curriculum and instruction.**

Points to Ponder

Create opportunities for volunteers to network with other volunteers, be involved in social activities, and be celebrated for their continued contribution. Providing volunteers with specific feedback about their performance will strengthen the role volunteerism plays in the school.

Ensure Success: Placing Volunteers Appropriately

Background

Volunteers are just that, volunteers. They are spending their own time to assist the school. Respect their commitment by consulting with them and adapting assignments to fit their schedule and time constraints. Keep in mind that the school should know in advance what it wants the volunteers to do and how it is to be accomplished.

Ideas to Use

83. Know volunteers as individuals.

Ask the following types of questions during an intake interview:

- What skills and talents do you possess that may not be readily apparent?
- What can we do to ensure that you feel welcome in the school?
- What were your experiences as a student?

SkyLight Training and Publishing Inc.

Volunteers who feel they are appreciated and valued as individuals as well as for their contributions will be strong advocates for the school.

84. **Consider the following factors when placing volunteers:**

- What kind of time commitment can the person make?
- How well does he or she relate to others?
- What skills or talents does the person possess?
- What are the possible frustrations or benefits of the different tasks assigned volunteers?
- What types of teaching styles exist in the placement situations?
- What has the past experience been with the volunteer?
- What are the preferences of the staff and the volunteers?

85. **Be responsible and accountable.**

Classroom teachers have responsibilities to their volunteers which include the following:

- Preparing an appropriate amount of work.
- Providing the directions and materials needed to do the assignment.
- Offering some variety in the tasks.
- Communicating expectations.
- Maintaining a schedule.
- Facilitating a full understanding of classroom routines, limits, and special needs.
- Showing appreciation.

86. **Provide staff with an in-service focusing on working effectively with volunteers.**

Teachers need to be reassured that volunteers will not comment on their teaching styles or personalities. If a problem does occur, the staff should have a mechanism in place to bring about an amicable resolution.

Points to Ponder

Some parents become disenchanted with volunteering when they are given less than involving tasks. Therefore, the placement of parents needs to be thought through to ensure that volunteers stay involved and committed. The worst public relations for a school is to have volunteers become disgruntled and cease volunteering. In addition, be clear about what the teaching and support staff union regulations say about the activities volunteers may perform.

Developing Collaborative Relationships

Background

> With frequent interactions between the schools, families, and communities, more students are likely to receive common messages from various people about the importance of school, of working hard and thinking creatively, of helping one another and staying in school.
>
> — *Joyce Epstein (1995, 702)*

Partnerships with community agencies, institutions, and organizations will give the school an increased sense of community and community identity. Collaboration provides the framework for action.

Ideas to Use

87. **Establish an art gallery in the school in cooperation with your local art club or association.**

Students can showcase their masterpieces in the school hallways along with that of local artists. This project creates the benefits of profiling the fine arts in school as well as being aesthetically pleasing. Local artists may even be inspired to donate pictures to the school for permanent display.

88. **Use the school as a student employment center.**

Offer student services such as painting, gardening, babysitting, and pet sitting. Use the school newsletter, Web site, and the local media to advertise the services. Have students prepare a résumé as part of the program.

89. **Involve the school in program registration for non-profit organizations.**

Guides, scouts, community colleges, and the local parks and recreation department may want to take the school up on its hospitality.

90. **Hold a summer reading exchange.**

Invite parents and students to swap both children's and adult books prior to the summer recess. Include materials from the school library that have been weeded from its collection.

91. **Support the season.**

Community service agencies need the support of schools to help fill their mandates, especially during the holiday season. Canvas businesses to determine what services they would provide to families in need (haircuts, dry-cleaning, and car repairs). Have students collect non-perishable foods and either prepare hampers or donate the foods to local charities for distribution.

92. **Host community services information evenings to inform your school community of available resources.**

Include information on adult education, health services, social services, and law enforcement. Link these evenings with other more traditional evenings such as Meet the Teacher night. It will not only help attendance but will demonstrate the positive relationship the school has with the community at large.

93. **Plan seminars for real estate agencies to introduce them to the schools in the district.**

94. **Always be prepared.**

There is a very valuable and essential role for parents to play in developing an emergency preparedness plan for home and school. Invite parents to hear guest speakers or to raise money to purchase emergency kits or a truck container to house earthquake and emergency supplies.

95. **Sponsor community forums.**

Community forums could include election debates (district, municipal, state or federal candidates); municipal issues such as bond issues, parks, roads, budget; school district issues such as literacy, truancy, or student retention.

96. **Establish a community information center that provides current information on local organizations and government; social services agencies, community events, and any other community resources.**

SkyLight Training and Publishing Inc.

Points to Ponder

The more opportunities provided for parents and community members to be in the school, the better. Support the use of the school as the center for the community as a whole. Create opportunities for the community to communicate how they can support the school and how the school can support them. The mutual support and respect will pay a long-term dividend to both the school and business community.

SkyLight Training and Publishing Inc.

Loud and Clear: Communicating Effectively

Background

Communication needs to be a two-way street. Ask parents what form of communication works best for them. Demonstrate the school's willingness to try different forms of communication to ensure that parent and student voices are being heard.

Ideas to Use

97. Be empathetic.

Try to understand the position of the other person, whether it is a parent or a student.

98. Keep an open mind.

Do not have the answer or try to solve the problem before all sides of the issue have been heard.

99. Provide opportunities for input.

Have a suggestion box posted in the school and encourage feedback from the parents, staff, students, and community. Use a telephone tree that operates on a systematic basis to seek as well as share information. Have a mechanism in place by which parents may contribute to the school's newsletter or Web site.

100. Seek and respond to parent and student input regarding the creation and updating of a student handbook.

This is a good collaborative project for students, parents, and staff.

101. Keep the lines of communication open.

Consider the method used to communicate with parents when there is a student issue. Teachers should evaluate their level of effective communication by asking themselves these questions:

- When did I last talk to his or her parent?
- Was it a positive or negative message?
- How do I convey the message that it is the issue and not the student that I want to discuss?

102. **Send home a monthly portfolio of students' work; include reminders of upcoming events.**

103. **Contact all parents by October.**

Ask parents what method they prefer to establish and maintain ongoing communication. Utilize e-mail, cellular telephones, and pagers when possible.

104. **Mail letters home occasionally outlining the student's progress; include praise and areas of growth.**

A letter home in late August could be used as a means to welcome students who are brand new to the school or simply welcome all students to their new grade.

105. **Invite parents and family members to a monthly or bi-monthly assembly to celebrate positive student behavior and achievements.**

Hand out certificates or an appropriate item such as a bookmark to acknowledge and reinforce positive student behavior.

Points to Ponder

Since teachers and not parents are the ones who initiate or express areas of interest or concern most often, it is important to consider how to effectively communicate on a regular basis. Students receive the message that the teachers and parents are partners in their education when the lines of communication are open.

SECTION FOUR

Working in the Classroom

When teachers make parent involvement part of their regular teaching practice, parents increase their interactions with their children at home, feel more positive about their abilities to help their children in the elementary grades, and rate the teachers as better teachers overall; and students improve their attitudes and achievement.

—*Joyce Epstein and Susan L. Dauber (1991, 289)*

Classroom teachers can either be stepping-stones or stumbling blocks to meaningful parent involvement. When teachers offer opportunities to parents to become involved in their child's education they are facilitating a meaningful partnership with parents. Conversely, when teachers do not offer specific strategies to parents or if they are too territorial of their classrooms, cooperation is brought to a halt. Educating students is a shared responsibility; therefore, it is essential that educators find ways to involve parents in the delivery of programs and services to students.

Supporting Specific Initiatives

Background

Provide parents with the opportunity to support programs that encourage both parent and student imaginations and energies in and out of school.

Ideas to Use

106. **Establish a specific timeline for the school read-a-thon that involves both parents and students.**

Start on a Monday and finish on a Monday. Set goals as a class for evening and weekend reading (ranging from 200 minutes for the primary students to 400 minutes for the intermediate students during a three-week stretch). Parents read to or read with their child during this time.

Have teachers and students prepare a progress report each Monday morning. Post a chart in the main hallway indicating the progress each class has made toward reaching their goal. Give all the parents and students who reach their reading goal by the end of the established time a certificate during a school assembly.

107. **Recognize student achievement in the community.**

Survey the parents and the business community to determine if students have accomplished something that would be appropriate to recognize at the school. Accom-

SkyLight Training and Publishing Inc.

plishments in the field of athletics, the fine arts, or volunteerism are among those appropriate to recognize.

108. Connect at a conference.

Have students, parents, grandparents, and teachers plan a full day conference to consider current issues such as the environment, effective communication, or the impact of technology. Select themes that can be offered to all delegates at the conference. Intersperse lectures and workshops with social activities such as a box lunch, family dance, or craft fair.

109. Spring into fitness.

Involve parents in working with students on increased physical fitness. Have students develop aerobic, rope skipping, or dance routines to be showcased at a school assembly. Focus on an overall healthy lifestyle by planning a "pot luck" supper featuring nutritionally sound fare.

110. Help form book discussion groups.

Open membership to students, parents, and the community at large. Intergenerational discussion provides students with adult perspectives other than those of their teachers and parents. It also serves to keep community members in touch with young people. Ask the advisory council to purchase a "book of the month" for the school library based on the selection made by the book group.

Points to Ponder

Decades of research have shown that by meaning-fully involving parents, student learning is strengthened; parents become advocates instead of adversaries, and all partners have a sense of ownership of public education (Henderson and Berla 1994).

SkyLight Training and Publishing Inc.

Higher than Intellect: Building Character

Background

Ralph Waldo Emerson once said that "character is higher than intellect" (Emerson 1837). Parents and schools are charged with cultivating the intellect as well as building character. By utilizing a parent/school partnership to provide opportunities for students to realize that their actions can influence others and in turn have an influence on the world, character and intellect are both strengthened.

Ideas to Use

III. **Sponsor a child from a developing country through groups such as UNICEF or the Red Cross.**

Make sure the funds needed for the sponsorship come from student fundraising efforts. Teach the students about where their child lives. Have classes study the culture, economics, and geography of their child's homeland.

II2. **Adopt a sister school.**

Have the school collaborate with a school in a different part of the town, state, province, or county to broaden understanding. Select a school in a different setting. A school in a big city could partner with a school in a rural area for example. Initial connections can be made teacher-to-teacher via the Internet. Plan visits, both day trips and overnighters, to expand the connections.

II3. **Develop student-mentoring programs at your school to build interpersonal connections among and between students.**

Mentors can help others with academic, social, or emotional support.

II4. **Implement a school-wide conserve energy and recycle plan.**

Integrate activities into school-wide themes. Offer incentives to classrooms that recycle. Have students use utensils from home for school events and lunches instead of using paper plates or polystyrene. Act as a recycling depot for the community. Call the local telephone company and participate in recycling telephone books. In addition to the positive effect on the environment, sponsoring paper and aluminum drives has the added benefit of raising money for the school.

II5. **Plant tulip bulbs on the school grounds (or at a local senior home) to commemorate Remembrance Day or some other important event.**

It is a good project for the advisory council to support financially.

II6. **Collect warm clothing, blankets, and sleeping bags for the homeless during the winter.**

Ask a local charity to help distribute.

Points to Ponder

Simple projects undertaken by teachers and students can promote social responsibility by having students care for the larger community. These activities provide students with opportunities to make charitable and meaningful contributions.

Creating Safe Havens for Students

Background

Appropriate attention to discipline and order help schools and parents provide a safe and sane environment for students. However, when school is not in session and parents are at work, unattended or improperly supervised young people can present a risk to themselves and their community. Therefore, coalitions must be built to provide for the safety of students during the school day and beyond.

Ideas to Use

117. Reach out to establishments in the community (such as ice and roller rinks, movie theaters, bowling alleys, and community libraries) that cater to student interests.

Find out if they are willing to donate space or develop programs during the school's non-instructional days. Ask the businesses what community service the students could offer in return.

118. Institute a "Plan Your Holiday" program.

Organize a program with parent volunteers for teenagers, aged fourteen and fifteen, for excursions such as backpacking, orienteering, hiking, and swimming.

SkyLight Training and Publishing Inc.

119. **Work with recreation services in the community to provide adult and youth summer programs, which could include gymnastics camp, movie matinees, crafts programs, and first aid instruction.**

Allow for the open use of school computers and library facilities. Provide physical education facilities for use by fitness programs.

120. **Offer summer programs for pre-schoolers at the school.**

Include activities such as games, crafts, storytelling, and educational video viewing. Meet two or three days a week for two hours a day. This provides for a stress-free introduction to the school building for parents and tots alike.

121. **Provide before- and after-school activities at the school for students who would otherwise be left home alone.**

122. **Have the noon-hour supervisors carry a clipboard with them as they supervise the grounds.**

When students do something worth recognition or if they have a problem, have the supervisors record it. Celebrate positive student behaviors such as leadership, cooperation, responsibility, and helpfulness. Be sure that the positives as well as the negatives are dealt with in a proactive fashion.

123. **Make school-wide discipline an annual goal that is widely discussed.**

All partners, including the students, should have input. Follow well-researched training programs that outline appropriate behavioral expectations based on accepted principles such as logical consequences. In addition, provide ongoing training to staff and parents to ensure the effectiveness of the plan once it has been implemented.

Point to Ponder

Collaborative efforts between the school, parents, and community can help ensure that students are safely and productively involved on days when not in school. Consequently, connections are forged or strengthened between the home, school, and community.

SkyLight Training and Publishing Inc.

High Finance: Fundraising

Background

Fundraising will always be a major role for staff and for parents. It is important that fundraising is not the only way in which parents are asked to volunteer their time. While it is a necessary function, it is only one of the many roles in the parent-school partnership.

Ideas to Use

124. **Employ typists.**

Have business education students offer their services to small businesses. Clients can drop off and pick up their typed pages daily.

125. **Create a cookbook for children.**

It could be the product of a classroom writing project. Ask parent volunteers to help with typing or desktop publishing the book.

126. **Feature graduating seniors in the school newsletter using their baby pictures.**

Sell these "congratulatory" photo ads to parents who can write the accompanying text. Use the funds for safe graduation celebrations.

127. **Invite families to decorate a gingerbread house in their own unique way.**

Also, ask local celebrities like teachers, the mayor, and the police chief to each decorate a house. Offer prizes for the most creative. Auction or raffle the gingerbread houses at holiday time.

128. **Hold a craft and bake sale.**

Rent tables to purveyors at $20 a piece. Be sure to require a deposit for each table prior to the event.

129. **Have students participate in a work-a-thon.**

This will not only raise funds but also provide a much need community service. Offer services, such as window washing, backyard clean up, and painting, at a minimal charge. Be sure that the senior citizens in your community have first access to student services.

130. **Host a fashion show.**

Work with local dress shops and have practical arts students model the clothes they made along with the ones from the retail shops. As part of the event, provide an opportunity for participants to try on and purchase the clothing with the school receiving a percentage of the resulting sales.

Points to Ponder

When parental help in raising funds is sought, be specific about what the funds will support. Funds collected by or through the help of parents and students help bridge the gap created by budget shortfalls and are increasingly important to the successful operation of many schools. Athletics, the arts, and enrichment programs in many cases could only be run with moneys received through fundraisers.

Talking Person to Person

Background

Parent-teacher conferences are often stressful for students, parents, and teachers alike. Prepare parents and students for the experience to ensure it is positive for all parties concerned. Let students be active partners in planning for the conference. Remember that parents have a right and a responsibility to be involved in their child's education. Expect parents to provide insights, seek clarification, and pose questions. Be open and honest.

Ideas to Use

131. **Keep parents informed about the curriculum covered between report cards and conference times.**

Discuss the instructional and assessment strategies used. Put as much as possible into written form (class newsletters, bulletins, or the Web site).

132. **Consider holding conferences in locations other than the school, such as at the student's home, a local restaurant, or in the community library.**

133. **Have the student help prepare for the conference either by filling out a form or by having a fellow student interview him or her.**

In either case, the student should answer the following questions:

- Do you enjoy school? Why or why not?
- What do you do best in school?
- Where do you want to improve?
- What work of yours would you like your parents to see?
- What is the best thing that has happened to you at school in the last year?
- Where have you improved the most?
- What will you do to help achieve your goals?
- How can your parents help you to succeed in school?

Points to Ponder

Use conference time as an opportunity to ask how parents feel about the school and its programs. Have a volunteer sign-up sheet handy. The parent-teacher conference should be viewed as a communication opportunity from both the parent's and the teacher's point of view.

Celebrating Diversity

Background

The manner in which a school addresses diversity is fundamentally demonstrative of the beliefs and values of that school community. Find ways to celebrate the variety of cultures in the school so that students can develop respect for others and conflict growing out of misunderstandings can be kept to a minimum.

Ideas to Use

134. Celebrate events such as *Gung Hey Fat Choy* (Chinese New Year), *Cinco de Mayo* (a Mexican victory celebration that dates back to 1862), or *Kwanzaa* (a "first fruit" festival deriving from African practices).

Integrate the celebrations as part of your multicultural studies curriculum. Any of these events can be celebrated through poetry, dance, food, works of art, or the study of the history and rituals around the festivals.

135. **Encourage families to host students from international exchange programs.**

It supports an understanding of other cultures and helps students learn more about their own country because they will serve as guides and teachers to their guests.

136. **Translate newsletters, notices, and other school and district information into the languages used in the homes of students.**

137. **Celebrate student heritage during an afternoon or evening event.**

Have students prepare for the event by selecting a culture they wish to study. Use print material, audio and video cassettes, and the Internet to gain information.

138. **Work with the local government office and sponsor a citizenship court or swearing in ceremony for new citizens.**

It benefits students, teachers, and new citizens.

139. **Support newcomers.**

Many communities have organizations that help new immigrants adjust to their adoptive country. Make contact with organizations, like the Traveler's Aid Society or a local faith-based organization, and determine ways to work with and support the organizations in their efforts.

Points to Ponder

As technology hastens the creation of a global society, there is a need to take every opportunity to appreciate and understand other cultures. The school can play a key role here by creating learning and teaching opportunities for students and adults in the school community.

SECTION FIVE

Venturing Beyond the Bake Sale

There is little agreement about how far parents can go in decision making or indeed what the impact of advocacy ultimately will be on the educational hierarchy. It seems obvious that there will be resistance in the educational establishment to sharing decision-making with parents.

—*Alan Riley (1994, 17)*

The success of public education is dependent upon public support. Consequently, educators must be responsive to students, parents, and the community at large in order to garner and sustain said support. Parents do not want to run schools, but they do want more shared responsibility in decision making. If the operational norms of a district are based on the principles of collaboration, consultation, and advice, then appropriate involvement of all partners is ensured.

Collaboration and Consultation: Setting Goals

Background

Schools all too often exclude parents from the goal setting process and simply announce what the goals of the school are. The challenge is to meaningfully involve parents in setting school goals. Once accomplished, the resultant combined pool of wisdom will ensure that better decisions are made. Parents will consequently be more supportive of steps taken to reach the goals because they were consulted on the formation of the goals in the first place.

Ideas to Use

140. **Allow parents direct input into the creation of the district and school's mission statements.**

Advisory councils and other parent groups should also define their missions and beliefs in this way. Creating a mission statement is the first step toward setting goals because the overall objective of an organization is then well defined. The statement then becomes the filter through which all school decisions must pass.

SkyLight Training and Publishing Inc.

141. SOCC it to them.

This activity could be done at an advisory council, a home and school association, or a joint meeting with the staff. List the Strengths, Opportunities, and Change to Consider (or S.O.C.C.). After each area is analyzed, regroup the participants and ask them to develop a three-year action plan that includes the following:

- Timeline over the three years with strategies prioritized
- Key Person(s) or group heading the campaign
- Budget implications
- Evaluation strategies
- Staff, parent, and student development activities.

The activity identifies the major areas of strength and the challenges faced by the school. Things that need to be changed or rethought are put into focus.

Points to Ponder

Goals and objectives must be "user-friendly," remembering that the users in many cases will not be trained educators but lay persons. The language as well as the depth and scope of the goals and activities must be realistic. All participants should have equal input into the decision to ensure that it is a product of collective thinking.

Measuring Up: Evaluating School Performance

Background

It is critical that the educational system be continually assessed. The process of evaluation must be seen as an opportunity for growth and development; therefore, the methods of evaluation should reflect this desire.

Ideas to use

142. **Establish formal ways the advisory council and the faculty can discuss and provide feedback to each other through joint meetings.**

If not feasible, have representatives attend each other's meetings and report back to their respective groups.

143. Understand the protocol.

Make parents aware of the appropriate procedure for evaluating the system. Be sure that staff is trained to react to parent concerns in a positive way. An accepted procedure for addressing parent grievances is to first discuss the issue or concern with the teacher or staff member involved. Then, if not resolved, discuss the situation with the principal. Make the names, office telephone numbers, and e-mail addresses of district personnel available to parents.

144. Perform an ABC evaluation at a parent and/or staff meeting.

Ask participants to finish the following sentences:
- A: Action that should be taken as a result of this meeting is . . .
- B: Best part of the meeting was . . . .
- C: Concerns I have are . . .

Points to Ponder

Remember that both parents and educators want the best for the students, and evaluation processes are a means to that end. Evaluation is simply a form of communication. Keep the lines of communication open, honest, and respectful between home and school.

Advice: Involving Those Affected by Decisions

Background

For the most part, educators believe in the positive implications of parent involvement. Most educators are comfortable with parents being involved and supportive of their child's achievement as well as with parents as volunteers in school. It is when parents want to become involved in decision making that parent involvement becomes a contentious issue. Educators are protective of their professional domain, while parents are demanding greater accountability and involvement. Achieving a balance between the partners' needs is the key to success.

Ideas to Use

145. Develop district-operating principles that support and encourage parents' involvement in decision making.

146. Ensure clear agendas at meetings by listing the topic, speaker, and time expected to cover the topic. Indicate whether the topic is limited or open for discussion. Provide opportunities for input into the agenda; perhaps at the end of each meeting, begin setting the agenda for the next. Set a deadline of three days prior to the meeting for additions to the agenda.

147. Make agendas for upcoming meetings available in advance.

Include the agenda on the district Web site or issue as a press release to the media.

148. Clarify decision-making procedures and who is going to be responsible for what actions.

149. Clearly define the problem or challenge.

Encourage open debate to elicit suggested solutions.

150. Establish a procedure that ensures that those affected by the decisions have an opportunity to be involved in the decision-making process.

Policies and procedures should not be set without completely analyzing the implications. Complete the advice cycle. (See The Advice Cycle diagram, Section One.)

Points to Ponder

Decisions that were once considered to be the domain of the educator are now a part of a shared governance mandate. Parents are very much a part of the new accountability movement, which is having a great impact on educational programs and services. Educators and parents need to learn to govern together because doing so will inevitably improve the quality of decisions.

Fostering Effective Advisory Councils

Background

Advisory councils are a formal group involved in school governance. The council should be involved in studying school issues, planning for improvements, and fostering positive school and community relationships. The key focus is to improve the quality of school life. Every school has an advisory council that includes parent representation. The mandates or names may change from place to place but societal expectations relating to school accountability remain the same.

Ideas to Use

151. **Revisit the purpose, belief statements, and mission statement of your advisory council to ensure it reflects the perspective of all the partner groups annually.**

It is important that advisory council members clearly understand their mandate. The clearly defined mandate needs to be articulated and shared not only with staff and parents but also with other social service agencies and the community at large.

152. Expand the membership of the council to include representatives from the community at large.

Representatives from business, industry, social service agencies, faith-based organizations, and local government should be sought out and invited to serve.

153. Set annual goals.

Provide all parents and staff with an opportunity for input. Include students in the goal-setting process where appropriate.

154. Give advance notice.

Set the schedule of meetings for the whole year. Arrange events and meetings during times when most parents can attend. This may result in having to schedule some during the day and some at night. Vary the day of the week meetings are held. Advertise council meetings prior to the event.

155. Be sure the agendas of the advisory councils are open and that the public has ample opportunity to place items on the agenda.

Make agendas public as far in advance of a meeting as possible.

156. Develop a system of communicating the outcomes of meetings.

This could be accomplished via newsletter, resource persons, bulletin boards, and Web sites or by broadcasting a videotape of the meeting on the community's cable access channel.

157. **Clarify the mandate of the council.**

Depending on the political setting, the council could be involved in staffing, budget preparations, curricular planning, facilities issues, and program evaluation.

158. **Have an education policy subcommittee as part of the advisory council.**

This group can provide feedback and input into proposed policies and procedures.

159. **Gauge the productivity and value of meetings by having a debriefing of the meetings immediately afterward.**

This could be done verbally or in written form.

160. **Establish operational norms for the meeting including rules of order and protocol.**

Points to Ponder

An effective advisory council will improve the trust, morale, and cohesion of the school community. The council should have both continuity and turnover in its membership, enough members to serve the needs of the school community, and meet with appropriate frequency.

SkyLight Training and Publishing Inc.

Developing Parent Potential

Background

Often educators use technical or professional jargon that functionally creates barriers to parent understanding of the educational system. Parents must be afforded avenues of inquiry into the current practices, research, and terminology specific to education. To this end, effort and priority must be given to the very real need for parent development so that parents can fully participate in the education of their children.

Ideas to Use

161. **Add a parent development strand to district staff development in-services.**

If the teaching staff is learning about proposed curriculum changes and teaching strategies, then host parallel sessions for parents. Promote the parent strand through school information organs. Ask parents to register either at their school or on-line to ensure that the proper accommodations can be provided.

162. Make parent development a regular part of advisory council meetings.

Designate a member of the advisory council to implement parent education programs. Open council meetings with a guest speaker or close them with an open forum on an education topic. Have faculty or administrative staff act as resource speakers or discussion facilitators.

163. Conduct a needs assessment to determine parents' needs and interests.

If possible, tie the assessment into social or community events. If there is a way to provide child care or involve students, then attendance will improve.

164. Form a district partners planning group that offers in-services on a variety of topics.

Plan four sessions per year on a district-wide basis. Address topics such as literacy, student discipline, budgeting, and vandalism.

165. Establish a parent library.

Allow parents access to the professional resource materials usually reserved for teachers. Collect print resources as well as video and audio tapes. Include materials on curriculum change, instructional strategies, and the latest research findings. Invite parents to come in and browse and borrow.

SkyLight Training and Publishing Inc.

166. **Host special sessions for parents and caregivers on topics such as:**

- How to help your child with homework
- The holistic development of the child
- Emergency preparedness
- Basic fire safety
- Study skills
- Drug and alcohol awareness

Be sure that the sessions are held when and where it is most convenient for the target audience, parents.

167. **Offer parenting workshops conducted by the school counselors on a variety of topics such as student discipline, coping with teenagers, and anger management.**

168. **Buy copies of the latest "read" in education and provide copies for the advisory council to circulate.**

Hold a book study session for interested parents.

169. **Call parents' attention to relevant parent resources, tips, and strategies for working with children on your Web site or newsletter.**

170. **Invite parents to drop in to the school on the way home from work to engage in some friendly conversation.**

Establish a routine and notify parents of what days administrators, school counselors, a specific grade level's group of teachers, or advisory council members will be available to chat. If the school has a track, invite the community to use the shower facilities after their respective daily runs.

171. **Plan "Advocates for Education" seminars.**

For example, if there is major change occurring in the district (decline or growth in student enrollment, reorganization of school models, new electives, boundary changes) train teams of speakers to present to the community. Invite parents to be part of the team and train them along with educators.

172. **Offer an annual parent conference through the district partnership committee or district advisory council.**

Schedule it for a Saturday between nine o'clock in the morning and two o'clock in the afternoon for the best chance at full participation. Charge a minimal fee to ensure attendance. Choose a topic that appeals to a variety of interests. Allow on-line registration. Advertise in the school and district newsletters and Web sites. Take advantage of free community announcements provided by local radio and cable stations.

Points to Ponder

Well-informed and educated parents make the best partners. Exploit every opportunity to inform and educate parents. Be sure to offer presentations that are appropriate to a variety of learning styles.

SkyLight Training and Publishing Inc.

District Initiatives: Setting the Example

Background

> The system must place a high value on openness, mutual respect, flexibility, responsiveness, and involvement. It must be attuned more closely to the following basic attributes: accessibility, relevance, diversity, achievement and accountability.
>
> —Barry Sullivan (Royal Commission Report 1988, 24)

District beliefs and operational principles must not only set policy for the schools in the district but must also set an example. Policy needs to center around offering sound educational programs and services to students in collaboration and consultation with parents.

Ideas to Use

173. Develop an annual district survey.

Use the first annual results as benchmarks to set standards for improvement.

174. Establish a standing district committee whose mandate it is to enhance and improve the quality of community relations.

Ensure that all the partner groups are represented on the committee.

175. As a district, expect that schools will have school councils with parent representatives.

176. Hold school board meetings and district forums in sites other than the board office.

Use community centers, faith-based sites, local schools, and city chambers.

Points to Ponder

Parental involvement is the cornerstone of any educational system. It must be made a priority in the district. Consequently, school-based practices will align with that of the district. Districts must model the concept that governance of a district is a community responsibility.

Appendix

WEB SITES FOCUSING ON INVOLVING PARENTS

Using all the popular browsers, more than 1,400 different Web sites were identified using the key words "involving parents." A significant number of the sites were reviewed with special attention being paid to the level of relevancy identified by the browser. (Snap and InfoSeek provided the most pertinent matches overall.) Those which best spoke to the issue of involving parents at all levels were selected, significantly reviewed, and appear here.

The sites' URLs (Uniform Resource Locators) appear for each as the Internet address. The Web protocol for each site is http://. In addition to domain names (as in the fictitious example *www.involvingparents.com*), subdirectory information is provided so that the user can obtain specific data. Information stored at a sites' subdirectory is separated from the domain name by a slash (as is the case with *www.involvingparents.com/resources*). Each site below was functioning at the stated URL as this book went to press.

Alliance for Parental Involvement in Education (ALLPIE)

www.croton.com/allpie/

The mission of this group and the objective of its Web site are to organize parents to make positive contributions to their children's education. Practical advice is offered.

British Columbia Teachers' Federation

www.bctf.bc.ca/bctf/parents/ParentsBr.html

Features of this site include a downloadable brochure detailing strategies for implementing parent involvement programs. You can conduct a search from their home page for other topics.

Community Access Program (CAP)

cap.unb.ca

A Canadian site offering information in English and in French about community-based programs as part of national partnerships that help garner access to technology for schools.

Communities in Schools

www.cisnet.org

Communities in Schools is a not-for-profit organization previously called Cities in Schools. Based in Alexandria, Virginia, the organization and its Web site offers down-to-earth ideas and conducts partnership classes for interested organizations. Whether or not Communities in Schools has a regional office in your area, they can provide help and direction to your programs.

SkyLight Training and Publishing Inc.

Family.com

www.disney.family.com

Affiliated with the Disney Company. Features of this
site include a searchable database. Click on Education
then type in "Involving Parents" to conduct your
search. Many interesting articles, including one from
the *Portland Parent,* "Getting Involved at Your Child's
School" and "45 Things You Can Do" both from a
parents' point of view are accessible through this site
as are general helpful hints to parents.

Hand in Hand

www.handinhand.org

Parents, Schools, Communities United for Kids, which
is sponsored by the Mattel Corporation, presents tips
and a downloadable brochure on how to affect parent/
school and community/school partnerships. The site
was designed in response to the National Education
Goals 2000 mandate to share information about
programs that expect, value, and nurture a family and
community role in children's learning.

Involving Hispanic Parents in their Children's Education

www.topher.net/~spurgeon/index.htm#school

An under-used, judging by its continuous count of
visitors to the site included on the home page, and very
valuable site. Marlene Spurgeon, a third grade ESL
teacher, outlines specific strategies for empowering
Hispanic parents. Ideas here can be applied to parent
populations in general but are especially good for
parents of language minority or disabled students.

Middle Web

www.middleweb.com

A site devoted to educational reform at the middle school level. Components of said reform include strategies for involving parents in their child's education.

National PTA

www.pta.org/programs/docs/involve.rft

Features a downloadable brochure on involving parents. From the home page find legislative updates and national standards of parent involvement in parent and family involvement programs. Includes teachers' best ideas for involving parents. Frequently updated.

Parent Soup: Education Central

www.parentsoup.com/edcentral/parentteacher/

This well-designed site is a tremendous resource for parents and teachers. It offers answers to the questions: Where can parents provide the most help? Great tips for parent/teacher cooperation and an on-line book *Parent Involvement in Education: A Resource for Parents, Educators, and Communities* are also among its offerings.

Pathway to School Improvement

www.ncrel.org/sdrs/pathwayg.htm

A cooperative effort between North Central Regional Educational Laboratory and the Regional Educational Laboratory Network. Provides current research and an audio journal from experts in the field of parent involvement. Excellent site with virtually up-to-the-minute information. Provides links to ERIC.

SkyLight Training and Publishing Inc.

Pennsylvania PTA

www.papta.org/parngoal.htm

Offers goals and objectives for parent involvement and other topical resources for parents and educators alike.

School Age

www.charleston.net/kids

A venture of the City of Charleston Public Schools, this site provides homework help with a wonderful reference desk for use by just about every level of student. On-line references, dictionaries, and thesaurus. Links to Library of Congress and other biggies of reference. A fundamental resource for parents helping with homework.

Strong Families, Strong Schools

eric-web.tc.columbia.edu/families/strong/index.html

The ERIC Clearinghouse on Urban Education for the U.S. Department of Education and the National Parent Information Network prepares the site. It provides meaningful things parents can do to help their children become successful learners and outlines methods for enlisting community involvement. Definitely a site worth visiting.

Teachers Helping Teachers

www.pacificnet.net/~mandel/

A site featured in *Education Week* and *Teacher Magazine* has had more than one million visitors since its inception in 1995. The teacher chat board is a good place to network and share ideas with other professionals about involving parents.

The Teachers Website

www.teachers.net

In addition to chat and lesson plans search this site for ever-changing implementation plans and ideas on how to bring about and utilize parent involvement.

SkyLight Training and Publishing Inc.

References

Bembry, J. X. 1996. "Impact of Volunteer Coordinators on Volunteer Programs." *Journal of Volunteer Adminstration,* 14 (2): 14-20.

Brandt, R. J. 1998. "Listen first." *Educational Leadership,* 55 (80): 25-30.

Emerson, R. W. August 31, 1837. "The American Scholar." An oration before the *Phi Beta Kappa Society,* at Cambridge.

Emmons, C. 1995. An interview with Christine Emmons on school climate. The SDP Newsline (on-line). Available: http//info.med.yale.edu/comer.

Epstein, J. L. 1995, "School/Family /Community Partnerships: Caring for the Children We Share." *Phi Delta Kappan,* 76 (9): 701-712.

Epstein, J. L. and Dauber, S. L. 1991. "School programs and teacher practices of parent involvement in inner-city elementary and middle schools." *The Elementary School Journal,* 91 (3): 289-304.

Fullan, M. G. 1991. *The new meaning of educational change.* 2d ed. New York: Teachers College Press.

Fullan, M. G. , and M. B. Miles. 1992. "Getting reform right: What works and what doesn't." *Phi Delta Kappan,* 73 (10): 744-752.

Goodlad, J. I. 1984. A place called school. New York: McGraw-Hill.

Henderson, A. T. and N. Berla, eds. 1994. *A new generation of evidence: the family is critical to student achieve-*

ment. Washington, D. C.: National Committee for Citizens in Education.

Iannaccone, L. 1975. *The Micro politics of education.* "Education policy systems: a study guide for school administrators." Fort Lauderdale: Nova University.

Joyce, B., J. Wolf, and E. Calhoun. 1993. *The self-renewing school.* Alexandria, VA: Association for Supervision and Curriculum Development.

Lewis, R. and J. Morris. 1998. "Communities for Children." *Educational Leadership* 55 (8): 34-36.

Lortie, C. 1975. "Speculations on change." *Schoolteacher: A sociological study.* Chicago: The University of Chicago Press.

Mandel, S. 1998. *Social studies in the cyberage.* Arlington Heights, IL: SkyLight Training and Publishing Inc.

National PTA. 1997. *National Standards for parent/family involvement programs.* Chicago.

Riley, A. 1994. "Parent empowerment: An idea for the nineties?" *Education Canada.* 34 (3): 14-20.

Sarason, S. B. 1990. *The predictable failure of educational reform.* San Francisco: Jossey-Bass.

Sullivan, B. 1988. *British Columbia Royal Commission on Education.* Victoria. British Columbia: Queen's Printer.

Treadwell, M. 1999. *1001 of the best Internet sites for educators.* Arlington Heights, IL: SkyLight Training and Publishing Inc.

Walberg, H. L. 1984. "Families as partners in educational productivity." *Phi Delta Kappan,* 65 (6): 397-400.

Zeigler S. 1987. *The effects of parent involvement on children's achievement: The significance of home/school links.* Toronto: Information Services Division of the Toronto Board of Education.

Index

ABC evaluation, performing, at parent and/or staff meeting, 89

Achievement. *See* Student achievements

Adult programs, offering, during school day, 32

Advice Cycle, 18, 91

Advisory councils
belief statements of, 92
clarifying mandates of, 94
education policy subcommittee as part of, 94
expanding memberships of, 93
fostering effective, 92–94
meetings of
agendas for, 93
communicating outcomes of, 93
establishing operational norms for, 94
gauging productivity and value of, 94
giving advance notice of, 93
making parent development a part of, 96

Advisory councils *(continued)*
mission statement of, 92
offering annual parent conference through, 98
providing feedback to, 88
purpose of, 92

"Advocates for Education" seminars, planning, 98

Agendas
for advisory council meetings, 93
ensuring clear, at meetings, 90–91
making available in advance, 91

Alliance for Parental Involvement in Education (ALLPIE), 102

Appreciation, showing, to volunteers, 23–24, 25

Art gallery, establishing, in school in cooperation with local art club or association, 60

Articulation meetings, offering, for parents of matriculating students, 31

Auction, holding blind, 51
Audit, inviting community
    members for, 30–31

Babysitting pools, facilitating,
    for volunteer parents, 22
Bake sale, holding, 78
Beautify the School plan,
    developing, 32
Blind auction, holding, 51
Book fairs, hosting, 9
Books
    and establishing of parent
        library, 96
    and establishing specific
        timeline for school read-a-
        thon, 68
    family reading night for, 9
    forming discussion groups for,
        69
    and promoting literacy, 9
Book study session, 97
British Columbia Teachers'
    Federation, 102

Caregivers, hosting education
    sessions for, 97
Car pools, facilitating, 22
Change
    affecting substantive, 40–42
    creating context for, 38–39
Character, building, 71–73
Childcare, providing free, for
    school activities, 21
Cinco de Mayo, celebrating,
    82–83
Citizens, swearing in ceremony
    for new, 83
Citizenship, modeling good,
    50–51
Citizenship court, sponsoring of,
    83
Class homepage, creating, 36

Classroom, working in, 67–84
Climate, creating, 29–47
Code of ethics, codifying, for
    volunteers, 54
Collaborative relationships,
    developing, 59–62
Color coordination of discus-
    sion, 28
Communication
    effective, 63–65
    empathy in, 63
    improved, as benefit of parent
        involvement, 3
    keeping lines of, open, 64
    on-going, with parents, 65
Communities in Schools, 102
Community
    establishing information
        center in, 61
    incorporating elements of,
        into curriculum, 52
    inviting members from, for
        audit, 30–31
    involving students in projects
        in, 32
    reaching out to establishments
        in, 74
    recognizing student achieve-
        ments in, 68–69
    sponsoring forums in, 61
    utilizing resources in, 50–53
Community Access Program
    (CAP), 102
Community service agencies,
    school support for, 60–61
Community services informa-
    tion evening, hosting at
    school, 61
Conferences
    connecting at, 69
    helping students prepare for,
        81
    holding, away from school, 80

SkyLight Training and Publishing Inc.

Conferences *(continued)*
  keeping parents informed
    between, 80
  offering annual parent,
    through district partner-
    ship committee or district
    advisory council, 98
Connections, establishing,
    45–47
Conversation. *See also* Commu-
    nication
  holding friendly, with parents,
    97
Cookbook, creating, 78
Coping with grief sessions,
    providing, 9
Craft sale, holding, 78
Curriculum
  incorporating elements of
    community into, 52
  integrating celebrations as
    part of multicultural
    studies, 82–83
  keeping parents informed
    about, 80

Decisions, involving people
    affected by, 90–91
Developing country, sponsoring
    child from, 71
District committee, establishing
    standing, to improve
    quality of community
    relations, 100
District forums, holding, at
    public sites, 100
District information, translating,
    into languages used in
    homes of students, 83
District partnership committee,
    offering annual parent
    conference through, 98
District partners planning
    group, forming, 96

District staff development in-
    service training, adding
    parent development
    strand to, 95–96
District survey, developing
    annual, 99
Diversity, celebrating, 82–84

Education
  fostering discussion about, as
    classroom teacher, 36
  hosting sessions in, for
    caregivers, 97
  hosting sessions in, for
    parents, 97
Education policy subcommittees
    as part of advisory
    council, 94
Emergency preparedness plan,
    developing, 61
Empathy in communication, 63
Energy conservation plan,
    implementing school-
    wide, 72
English as Second Language
    (ESL) classes, offering to
    community, 9
Enrollment information pack-
    age, preparing, 33
Ethics, codifying code of, for
    volunteers, 54
Extra-curricular clubs, finding
    volunteer coaches for, 50

Faculty. *See* Teachers
Families
  involvement of, at start of
    school year, 6–7
  supporting whole, 8–10
  surveying, to identify expertise
    in school community, 7
Family.com, 103
Family goods exchange, spon-
    soring, 9

Family literacy, promoting, 9
Family reading night, 9
Fashion show, hosting, 78–79
Feedback, providing to advisory council and faculty, 88
Field trips, visiting parents' job sites on, 52
Fill in the blank activity, 17
Fundraising, 77–79

Gingerbread house, decorating, 78
Goals
  parent involvement in setting, 86–87
  setting annual, for advisory councils, 93
  setting, collaboration and consultation, 86–87
Grief, providing coping with, sessions, 9
Grievances, redress of parent and student, and access to records, 2
Group activities, optimum size for, 20
Gung Hey Fat Choy (Chinese New Year), celebrating, 82–83

Halloween night, organizing safety patrols on, 52
Hand in Hand, 103
Hats off activity, 17
Homeless, collecting clothing, blankets, and sleeping bags for, 72
Home visits, 7

Ideas, facilitating full and free exchange of, 16–20
Immigrants, helping to adjust to adoptive country, 83

Individuals, knowing volunteers as, 56–57
Initiatives, for districts, 99–100
Initiatives, supporting specific, 68–70
International exchange programs, encouraging families to host students from, 83
Involvement, sustaining, 49–65
Involving Hispanic Parents in their Children's Education, 103

Job sharing, offering, 12
Job site field trips, 52

Kwanzaa, celebrating, 82–83

Letters, mailing home, 65
Life events, affect of, on attitudes, 41

Marketing the message, 34–37
Media, establishing contact with local, 35
Meetings
  of advisory councils
  agendas for, 93
  communicating outcomes of, 93
  establishing operational norms for, 94
  gauging productivity and value of, 94
  giving advance notice of, 93
  making parent development a part of, 96
  ensuring clear agendas at, 90–91
  holding school board, at public sites, 100

SkyLight Training and Publishing Inc.

Meetings *(continued)*
inviting parents and family members to monthly or bi-monthly, 65
offering articulation, for parents of matriculating students, 31
performing ABC evaluation at parent and/or staff, 89
Message, marketing the, 34–37
Middle Web, 104
Mid-year transfers, welcoming, 32
Mission statements, parent input into creation of, 86
Multicultural studies curriculum, integrating celebrations as part of, 82–83

National PTA, 104
Needs assessment, conducting, to determine parents needs and interest, 96
Newsletters
acknowledging and profiling parent volunteers in, 24
attaching "Beefs and Bouquets" section to, 18
featuring graduating seniors in, 78
publishing and circulating classroom, 36
translating, into languages used in homes of students, 83
Non-profit organizations, involving school in program registration for, 60

On-going communication, with parents, 65
On-going training, providing, for volunteers, 55

Operational system, role of parent in, 2
Orientation session, hosting, for volunteers, 54

Parent Boosters Club, 13
Parent comments
responding to, 36
soliciting, 35
Parent conference, offering, annual, through district partnership committee or district advisory council, 98
Parent get-togethers, facilitating, 10
Parent grievances, redress of, and access to records for, 2
Parenting workshops, offering, 97
Parent involvement
benefits of, 3
key to, 5
and student achievement, 2
Parent library, establishing, 96
Parent meeting, performing ABC evaluation at, 89
Parent representatives on school councils, 100
Parent Soup: Education Central, 104
Parents
calling attention to relevant resources, 97
developing potential in, 95–98
encouraging involvement of, in decision making, 90
hosting education sessions for, 97
input of, into district and school's mission statements, 86

Parents *(continued)*
  involving
    in goal setting process, 86
    in school read-a-thon, 68
    in working with students on increased physical fitness, 69
    motivating to remain involved, 14
    random seating of, in group, 43–44
    surveying, on topics, 36
    visiting job sites on field trips, 52
    web sites focusing on involving, 101–6
    welcoming of, as equal partners, 1–2
Pathway to School Improvement, 104
Pennsylvania PTA, 105
Perceptions as key to accepting change, 40
Personal contact, use of, to inform parents of volunteer opportunities, 12
Person-to-person communication, 80–81
Photomontage, assembling, 35
Physical atmosphere, creating friendly, 30
Physical fitness, involving parents in working with students on increased, 69
Pizza night, organizing, 51
Plan Your Holiday program, instituting, 74
Portfolio, sending home monthly, 65
Positive image, projecting, 30–33
Pre-schoolers, offering summer programs for, 75

Problem, clearly defining, 91
Protocol, understanding, for evaluations, 89
PTA, 13
Public representatives on school councils, 100

Random seating, 43–44
Real estate agencies, planning seminars for, 61
Recreation services, working with, in providing summer programs, 75
Recycle plan, implementing school-wide, 72
Red Cross, sponsoring child from developing country through, 71
Refreshments, providing to volunteers, 22
Remembrance Day, commemorating, 72
Resource directory, creating, 52

Safety patrol, organizing, on Halloween night, 52
School
  developing emergency preparedness plan for, 61
  hosting community services information evening at, 61
  involving, in program registration for non-profit organizations, 60
  planning real estate seminars at, 61
  planting tulip bulbs on grounds of, 72
  sponsoring community forums at, 61
  as student employment center, 60

SkyLight Training and Publishing Inc.

Index

School *(continued)*
support of, for community service agencies, 60–61
School activities
providing before- and after-, 75
providing free childcare for, 21
School Age, 105
School board meetings, holding, at public sites, 100
School community, becoming member of, 19
School councils, parent representatives on, 100
School information, translating, into languages used in homes of students, 83
School performance, evaluating, 88–89
School read-a-thon, establishing specific timeline for, 68
School-wide discipline as goal, 75–76
School year, involvement of families at start of, 6–7
Senior citizens, offering free admission for, to school events, 51
Senior members, adopting, 51
Sister school, adopting, 71–72
Staff meeting, performing ABC evaluation at, 89
Strengths, Opportunities, and Change to Consider (S.O.C.C.), 86–87
Strong Families, Strong Schools, 105
Structured approach, use of, in involving parents, 12
Student achievements
increased, as benefit of parent involvement, 3

Student achievements *(continued)*
and parent involvement, 2
recognizing, in community, 68–69
Student employment center, use of school as, 60
Student grievances, redress of, and access to records for, 2
Student handbook, including parent input in, 64
Student heritage, celebrating, 83
Student-mentoring programs, developing, 72
Students
celebrating positive behaviors, 75
creating safe havens for, 74–76
enhanced self-esteem as benefit of parent involvement, 3
helping prepare for conference, 81
involving, in school read-a-thon, 68
Suggestion box, 64
Summer programs
offering, for pre-schoolers, 75
reading exchange as, 60
working with recreation services providing, 75
Support group for single parents, fostering, 10

Teachers
providing feedback to, 88
responsibilities of, to volunteers, 57
Teachers Helping Teachers, 105

SkyLight Training and Publishing Inc.　115

Teachers Website, The 106

Team building, 26–28

Thank you notes, sending personalized, to volunteers, 24

Time capsule, 41

Training
adding parent development strand to district staff development in-service, 95–96
providing on-going, for volunteers, 55

Transportation alternatives, offering to parents without cars, 22

Traveler's Aid Society, 83

Treasure hunt, conducting human, 27

Tulip bulbs, planting, on school grounds, 72

Twenty questions, playing, 46–47

Typists, employing, 77

UNICEF, sponsoring child from developing country through, 71

Venn diagram in initiating discussion about change, 41–42

Video, creating, starring school, 33

VIP buttons, use of, for volunteers, 24

Volunteer coordinator, employment of, 13

Volunteer fair, 13

Volunteer handbook, developing, 55

Volunteer of the month or week, recognizing, 24

Volunteers
acknowledging contributions from, 23–25
advertising for, 11–12
codifying code of ethics for, 54
evaluating performance and giving appropriate feedback, 15
factors in placing, 57
hosting orientation session for, 54
involving in planning, evaluating, and implementing programs and projects, 14
knowing, as individuals, 56–57
meeting needs of, 14–15
placing, appropriately, 56–58
providing on-going training for, 55
providing refreshments to, 22
recruiting, 11–13
responsibilities of classroom teachers to, 57
supporting, 21–22
team building with, 26–28
training, 54–58
using to distribute programs, bulletins, and newsletters in school neighborhood, 35
working effectively with, 58

Web sites
creating classification of homepage as link from, 36
featuring parent volunteers and their contributions on, 24
focusing on involving parents, 101–6

SkyLight Training and Publishing Inc.

Welcome package, preparation and distribution to new families, 6–7

Work-a-thon, students participation in, 78

Yearbook, acknowledging and profiling parent volunteers in, 24